Rise Slay Eat

# Rise Slay Eat

## Practical Ways In Becoming The Best Version of Yourself

### Robert L. Wagner

*P.H.A.T.B.O.Y. Music
and Publishing
Fort Worth, Tx*

Copyright © 2021 Robert L. Wagner.

All rights reserved. No part of this book may be used or reproduced by any means, graphic, electronic, or mechanical, including photocopying, recording, taping or by any information storage retrieval system without the written permission of the publisher except in the case of brief quotations embodied in critical articles and reviews.

Because of the dynamic nature of the Internet, any web addresses or links contained in this book may have changed since publication and may no longer be valid. The views expressed in this work are solely those of the author and do not necessarily reflect the views of the publisher, and the publisher hereby disclaims any responsibility for them.

# Contents

Introduction   1

1. Get Your Mind Right   5
2. Know Thyself - Self Awareness   11
3. Personal Temperature Gauge   17
4. Be Good To Yourself: Self Love   23
5. Embrace Your Uniqueness   27
6. Friends, How Many Of Us Have Them?   33
7. Forgiving Yourself   41
8. Creating Clarity: Life Mapping   45
9. Set On Fire   51
10. Healthier Life Journey   55
11. Serve Others   59
12. Refueling (Rest)   63
13. Center S.T.A.G.E.   71
14. Be Adventurous: Life Is Good   79

About The Author   81

Miracle, over the past 12+ years, I have learned a great deal of becoming more authentic due to you. Thank you for loving the raw and uncut and pushing me toward greatness.

To Mom/Dad, who always stressed, "no one can do what you do like you do it." I learned a great deal about authenticity from you both and being true to one's self.

## NOW IT'S YOUR TURN

SE7EN University, is an interactive online training program that leads people to self-mastery.

Join others at SE7EN U with our on-demand audio, email and video teachings leading people to self-mastery. SE7EN University "Leading People to self-mastery"

Whether you need help in personal, leadership, or

spiritual development, SE7EN University will challenge you to grow and become the best version of yourself possible. I invite you to join others with our on-demand audio, email, and video teachings leading people to self-mastery.

## Testimonials

"God has uniquely created and purposed you to take the leading role in your life. If you're ready for true change but not sure where to begin, *Rise, Slay, Eat* is a powerful way to make a head start on your journey."
– **Dr. QuaVaundra Perry**, Christian psychologist and author of The Emotion Devotional

"Captivating and inspiring read from beginning to end. I couldn't put Rise Slay Eat down until the last chapter. Robert takes you on a journey of self discovery to assist in shaping your authentic zeal for life. You'll find encouragement, practical examples, and the determination to plow forward in your endeavors."
– **Miracle L. Wagner**, Licensed Professional Counselor Owner & CEO ~ Miracle Works, PLLC

"As a founder of a non-profit organization, this book was right on time for me. I often struggle with feeling inferior to other organizations. In the chapter *Embrace Your Uniqueness*, I learned that I must stop comparing myself to others and compare myself to me. Another nugget I received was from the chapter, *Be Good To Yourself*. It made me realize I must acknowledge the accomplishments I've already achieved, whereas I've often overlook those significant accomplishments in times past. This book has shown me areas where I can improve, and if a person applies the tools given in this book, they will see their lives changed for the better."

**– Monica Hall**, Founder of I Was Once U

"Rise Slay Eat will give you what is needed to 'burn in such a way that you attract others.' Robert L. Wagner confrontshabitual patterns that extinguish rather than ignite and gives readers practical, proven practices to enkindle the fire within."

**– Fred Willis**, Digital Media Entrepreneur

"Everything comes with a manual except the mind. Transformation comes from within. Rise, Slay, Eat is one of the dopest, thought provoking books I've read since this pandemic. The author of this book has carefully crafted the basic fundamentals of living a sustainable lifestyle."

**– Tina R Williams**, MBA, CLC
CEO/ Posh Entertainment Brand Management Firm

"I have read a lot of books that inspire and motivate me. But, I love books that give you a practical step-by-step guide to improvement. If you're looking for an all-in-one guide that literally covers everything. Rise Slay Eat is for you."

– **Brent Butler**, Pastor
Eastside Community Church

# INTRODUCTION

Although it appeared that I was effortlessly confident as a young man, it wasn't an easy road. I had my fair share of self-image mishaps and struggles. There were and are things I didn't like about myself, but those things never hindered me from moving forward.

Growing up, I would hear the words "nobody can do what you do like you do it" echoing from my parents' mouths. I believe there was a level of confidence and purposeful living instilled in me from an early age. Now granted, this is a combination of nature and nurture. However, I walk into whatever room knowing who I am and whose I am because I live authentically and I'm becoming the best version of myself daily.

Rise Slay Eat will take you on a practical journey to becoming more authentic. To live authentically is to burn in such a way that attracts others. However, it is a process that results in newfound self-awareness and courage to create a life that genuinely makes you proud.

This book is a journey that begins with developing the mindset of a champion. Only after setting the right attitude can we move to know ourselves a little better by being self-aware. The path continues by establishing our temperature gauge through core values and being good to yourself through self-love. As we know, we are all unique individuals, and the next step is to embrace that individuality. Even though we are unique individuals, we are not called to live on an island without others, so we will look at friendships. Creating a clear map for your life is found in the next chapter, and then we set ourselves on fire. When we are on fire, let's continue with a healthier journey and realize that life is not just about us but how we use what we have to serve others. Finally we can take Center S.T.A.G.E. of our lives and live adventurously.

Working in the field of social services for over a decade and as a strategic leader, I have seen that change is generally deficient in life because of three failures:

- Failure to see.
- Failure to set things in motion.
- Failure to sustain that which we have put in motion.

Although confident, the things I didn't like about

myself never stopped my journey. I mustered up enough courage to work on them while moving forward, and I am still working on them. I desire that as you read this book, you can also muster up enough courage to work on yourself and become the best version of yourself possible.

### Here's an action item:

This book is filled with a lot of practical steps and things to wrestle with. The action today is to grab a journal and begin to jot down your thoughts throughout this book. Start now with what you desire to gain from this book.

# 1

# Get Your Mind Right

Have you noticed that affirmations are everywhere? From books to social media posts to words on a desk, affirmations are a part of life. They have the unique ability to change our thinking and lift our spirits. They have the power to change your thoughts, self-talk, and ultimately, your actions. They can strengthen your talents and help you develop traits that you wish to learn. They can enable you to overpower negative thoughts with positive ones and develop a champion's mindset.

A champion mindset is from a place of victory, not a

victim. One of the most famous Psalms is found in the 23rd chapter. There is a great scene where David states, "though I walk through the valley of the shadow of death, I will fear no evil, for you are with me." A victim's mindset sees the valley and sees the death. However, a champion knows that there are highs and there are valleys. The valley you may currently be in is not the destination, but you walk through it. The death you may feel around you is only a shadow, and there is no need to fear because He is with you.

When you change your thinking process, everything in life changes. Paul Carlin once said, "people do what they do because they believe what they believe." Each day, thousands of thoughts cross our minds, and choosing positive affirmations can rewire our brains. They create a new focal point and change the way we think. Every thought makes a burst of neurochemicals in our brains. As a result, patterns are formed in our brain, and something powerful happens; emotions are attached to each thought resulting in action.

Affirmations help us to keep a positive attitude about life. There are many places to find affirmations; but one powerful tip is writing your own.

**When you start writing your own affirmations, keep these tips in mind:**

1. Make them personal. There is extreme value in

using I; after all, these should be unique to you (Ex: "I am worthy!")
2. Use the present tense. An effective affirmation should be designed to change your subconscious and feelings now, which is why it's imperative to keep them focused on the moment at hand. My father used to say, "when we focus on the past, we get depressed; when we focus on the future, we get anxious, focus on the present."
3. Be Precise. Although there is value in longer affirmations, most affirmations are meant to be short and sweet.
4. Make it positive. Although useful at times, try to avoid using negative words like not, but work on positive statements that will motivate you to grow.

## Believe in the Power of Affirmations

As you confess your affirmations, believe them to be true. Affirmations are compelling sets of words as long as you believe what you're telling yourself. Remember they have a way of rewiring your brain.

As you set your eyes on your goal, write positive affirmations that will help motivate you along the way. It is also important to keep your affirmations in a place where you can see them constantly, and repeat them often.

Affirmations can make all the difference in reaching your goals. Give them a try and enjoy the benefits these positive statements can make in your life.

## Here's an action item:

Practice makes better and it's important to rehearse these affirmations daily. Affirmations can make a huge difference, so start writing these affirmations in your journal. The one that resonates most, write it 25 times each day for week; Live it, breathe it, Be it!

### Affirmation Starters

1. I love myself.
2. I am incomparable.
3. I deserve to be cherished.
4. I am compassionate and full of love.
5. I am willing to begin with an open mind and heart.
6. I am worthy.
7. I am strong and confident.
8. I am in control of my fears.
9. I allow myself to shine bright.
10. I enjoy living in the moment.
11. I learn from my mistakes.
12. I live a worry-free life.
13. I am purposeful.

14. I am fearless.
15. I am competent.
16. I will succeed.
17. Today, I manifest my dreams.
18. I am satisfied with who I am becoming.
19. Regardless of what happens today, I will think positively.
20. I value my peace.
21. I have the power to set appropriate boundaries.
22. It's okay to be assertive.
23. I will achieve my goals.
24. I will do my best.
25. I can do anything I put my mind to.
26. I reward myself.
27. I define my success.
28. My failures are not useless; they teach me what to do differently.
29. I will not let fear prevent me from trying.
30. I am stronger today because of yesterday's mistakes.

# 2

# Know Thyself – Self Awareness

Taking the step towards becoming the best version of yourself requires a crucial step towards self-awareness. However, developing your self-awareness is a journey. There's no quick fix. People who reach high levels of success in personal and professional areas tend to share a key trait: self-awareness.

## What is self-awareness?

Self-awareness is the discovery and the ability to take an honest look at yourself. Webster defines it as "an awareness of one's own personality or individuality." Those who have self-awareness have a clear understanding of self: strengths, temperament, abilities, gifts, and experiences. They know what makes them tick or what shapes them. Studies have suggested that when we increase self-awareness, our confidence and creativity become more robust. If you want to develop your leadership skills, enhance your career progression, or focus on your personal development, building self-awareness is critical. It is also vital to be self-aware to know how others perceive you. When was the last time you had a conversation with a friend or spouse and discovered that you saw the same situation in two different ways? The answer is perspective. Everyone has their view, individual opinions, values, ideas, etc.

Looking at situations from other points of view is one of the most effective ways to enhance your self-awareness. It will broaden your perspective, allowing you to see alternative opinions and opportunities. It's tough to be self-aware without stepping outside of your view of the world. When you lack self-awareness, life can be frustrating, relationships can become broken, and your career stagnant.

An unskilled person or unaware individual has the following traits:
- Doesn't know self well – strengths, weaknesses, etc
- Doesn't seek feedback – possibly defensive or arrogant.
- May over/underestimates their performance.
- Avoid discussions about self.
- May become a person who blames others, doesn't learn from mistakes.

However, a skilled person:
- Knows strengths
- Seeks feedback
- Open to criticism and not defensive
- and gains insights from mistakes.

It serves us well to understand self-awareness and some critical identifiers of a skilled and unskilled person. Still, when it comes to applying strategies to enhance self-awareness, you need practical tips.

## Strategies to be more self-aware

The first strategy you should start with is creating the habit of reflection. Have you ever taken time to think about the significant areas of your life? What do you value? This could include things like your marriage, friendship, career, business, education, etc. Take time to write down a list of the most important things to you. After you have written them down, on a scale of 1-5, how would you rank where you are in each area? Once you have written these areas out and ranked them, ask yourself these three questions; first, how would I like these areas to improve? Secondly, what steps do I need to take to improve these areas? Thirdly, how will I know when I start making progress? The second strategy is to seek feedback. People are usually reluctant to give you negative feedback. To receive it, you must ask for it. When we seek negative feedback or corrective information, it increases both our overall effectiveness and the accuracy of our understanding. A great way to gain feedback from others is to do so in a confidential manner. Often called 360 surveys, they tend to be more accurate because people generally stray from negative thoughts in public. Because different people know us in different ways, it is also helpful to seek feedback from multiple sources. When receiving feedback, you will see three specific areas:

**Truth Spots** – things people see that are true about you

**Blind Spots** – what others see that you don't but are true

**Perceived Spots** – what others think they see but are not true

The last strategy in becoming more self-aware is becoming more humble. Generally, prideful people don't want feedback, or when it is given, they tend to become defensive or angered. Prideful individuals tend to overvalue, overrate, or overestimate themselves. However, humility is having an accurate view of yourself.

Remember, this is a journey, not a sprint. It is a process that takes effort. No matter where you are on the self-awareness scale, you can always be developing. You can still be learning more about yourself. As you start making progress towards self-awareness, I would like to introduce a slightly different take on S.M.A.R.T. goals. First, ensure the improvement is *specific*. Be specific with the area in need of growth and how you want to grow it. Secondly, be *measurable* (success criteria). To evaluate the development or lack thereof, you must have a success criterion. Third, it needs to be *attainable*. Just like any goal, progression is critical. Ensure that your dreams of improvement are attainable (possible). Fourth, it needs a *"required" support system*. Don't go at this alone. Everyone needs a support system to grow and also see blind spots. Lastly, *time-based*. As you are writing out your developmental plan, have a specific date in mind as a target.

## Here's an action item:

Spend some time reflecting on yourself. Do you see any patterns in your thoughts/feelings? Next, begin to work through your S.M.A.R.T. goals.

### Personal Affirmation

I am on the path towards self-discovery. As I become more self-aware, I will strengthen my relationships, and they will be easier to manage. I understand who I am and respect the opinions of those seeking to bring me good. I know there is no quick fix; this is a journey that I am willing to embark on. I will develop my leadership skills, enhance my career progression, and focus on my personal development; because building self-awareness is critical.

# 3

## Personal Temperature Gauge

I was inside my friendly neighborhood Walmart, and after grabbing some groceries, I made my way to the checkout. Although it was quicker to go through the self-checkout line, it is always more fun to talk to an actual person. After having conversation with the cashier and receiving my change, I noticed she gave me a little too much back, $20 too much. At this moment, a decision is made by many of us; some of us would think "God made a way", and others will think she overpaid me, and I don't want her drawer to come up short.

What we value will be determined by the decisions we make in those critical moments.

I have launched a few initiatives throughout my life. Whether it was an organization, a team, or a business, one key to success was the groundwork in preparing for the launch. Because values are like guiding stars, each launches' success depended heavily on the values that were laid out. When we know our values and live by them, our lives become simpler and more enjoyable.

Values are the temperature gauge by which everything flows. They give us direction as to how we want our lives or organizations to navigate troubled waters. Many organizations have core values somewhere listed; many of us are even aware of the values that identified our families. However, how many of us are aware of the values that dictate our lives?

One way to honestly know yourself is to get in touch with your own set of values.

It's effortless to be sidetracked or distracted by the ideas of others. So often, we hijack what's right for others and apply them to ourselves when faced with difficulty. However, it is highly vital to know the things that are important to you. In essence, your values are the things that are most important to you at the core. It's the unwavering belief in what you stand for. When you know your values, you can live an authentic life doing what's most important to you.

Yet, most people have never taken the time to discover what's important to them. Therefore, when life hits, we sail with convenience. Before long, we look up, and our lives have gone by, and we feel inauthentic because we lived a life based on what's important to others and not ourselves. But it is never too late to discover what's important to us, and we can start today.

## Identifying Values

A practical method of identifying your values is to imagine your future. Take the time to reflect on different areas of your life. Where do you see yourself as you get older? What are the things that are most important to you? What do you hope to accomplish in life, and how would you want to be remembered?

Answering these questions will help you discover your values. For instance, if you picture yourself growing old close to your family and spending valuable time with your grandkids, then a strong sense of family is one of your core values.

You can have many values in life; you just need to discover your highest priorities. That way, at the end of each day, you can feel confident that you're nurturing the essential parts of your life. Again, taking center S.T.A.G.E. in your life is predicated on knowing what you value.

## Popular Values

To help you get started, here is a list of a few popular values.

| | | |
|---|---|---|
| **Family** – caring for loved ones | **Security** – being free of danger | **Creativity** – innovation |
| **Spirituality** – focusing on faith and intangibles | **Belief** – trust in someone/ something | **Integrity** – sincerity, honesty |
| **Leadership** – having influence with people | **Health & Wellness** – well-being | **Teamwork** – focusing on collaboration |

All you need to do to discover your values is find what makes you truly alive. Then ask yourself why those things bring you joy. The answers will help lead you to your core values.

Many times in counseling or coaching others, people feel like their lives have taken a wrong turn. If you think this way, you can figure it all out by thinking about your future. Are you helping your future self by walking down your current path? If the answer is no, perhaps it's time to think about taking a new approach based on your core values. When you do, that path will likely lead you to happiness!

## Here's an action item:

Let's discover our values. What makes you alive? Happy? How do you see yourself? From the list, what resonates with you? What do you think your values are?

### Personal Affirmation

I know who I am and what is important to me. My values keep me grounded and direct my decisions. Learning and living my values make life simpler and more enjoyable. I am clear about my values; therefore, I can be more thoughtful and less reactive.

Like a compass, my values help direct my decisions by bringing clarity and certainty. My life is more comfortable to navigate because I choose to be the living embodiment of my values.

My values make it easy for me to make decisions. Whenever I feel indecisive, I return to my values, and the best choice becomes clear. Decisions are only challenging when I forget or ignore my values.

Today, I choose to be guided by my values. I free myself of the burden of living outside of them. I allow my values to guide my decisions and behavior.

# 4

# Be Good To Yourself: Self Love

In order to become the best version of yourself possible, it is vital to love yourself. And to love yourself, you must accept who you are, flaws and all. You want to feel comfortable showing yourself to the world. I believe that self-acceptance is the first step in building confidence and self-love.

Now don't be deceived into thinking that you can't love yourself but are dissatisfied with where you are currently in life. You may be unhappy with the path you have taken, but it's okay. You are human. You can't get to where you already think you are. I guess it happens to everyone, but that is why we fight for more.

Remember that you are unique, and no one can take your place in this world. Accepting yourself for who you are can also boost your confidence and help you take advantage of your innate skills for your benefit and others.

Try these three strategies to achieve contentment and love yourself.

## Remember you are an anomaly

You are unique, and it's important to know that you are not a mistake. Although the process to conceive may have been accidental, your conception is a work of pure genius. Out of the 100s of million soldiers that marched or swam uphill, you made it. You are not a mistake, and the very presence of your existence means you are a conquerer.

## Consider your accomplishments

I bet you have achieved a lot of things throughout life, both personally and professionally. A lot of times, we gloss over these achievements. As a leader, I love keeping a significant event log for those I serve. It is always astonishing when preparing someone for an interview how they minimize or forget the outstanding accomplishments they have achieved. Just like an employee getting ready for an interview, we often forget about our accomplishments. These accomplishments all took place in your life. You accomplished them with your strength, temperament, abilities, gifts, and experiences, and you are a person of influence and the champion of your story, and no one can take those victories away from you.

## Avoid minimizing yourself

When we underestimate ourselves, it can lead to unhappiness because we are unhappy with where we are in life. What we don't prioritize gets minimized. Often the reason you don't have what you want is that you haven't tried to get it. Begin to prioritize yourself and progress towards your goals; progress towards your goals begins when we are clear of where we are currently.

- Don't miss your opportunity to reach your goals worried about your opposition. Stop worrying about others and wishing you had what they have; you have all that you need within you to achieve greatness; create a plan of action to get what and where you want.

- Have a strong commitment that nothing separates you from your goals. You won't leave where you are until you decide it's not where you want to be. You have what it takes to reach them, so keep pressing.

You were uniquely created with the talents and skills to have a fulfilling life, not a life of regrets!

## Here's an action item:

Journal one thing that you are dissatisfied with within your life. Reflect on what the silver lining for this situation could be. Write a detailed plan for how you could change this situation for the better.

### Personal Affirmation

I am fearfully and wonderfully made. I am the star of my story and I deserve to be loved. I am worthy. Life doesn't have to be perfect to be great, and yet I wake up and smell the roses. I live without regrets. I embrace my individuality and celebrate differences. Today, I choose me!

# 5

## Embrace Your Uniqueness

During my college years, I stumbled upon a store at a local mall. It was a leather store, and I found something that I knew instantly I had to get. If you saw any of my latter-year college photos, chances are you saw this item during the winter. Someone started the process of getting a leather jacket made but never came to finish it. Ironically, the measurements were almost identical to mine, and after a few tweaks, I purchased the coat. It was sleek, stylish, and custom, well semi-custom.

It was my first semi-custom product. Since that time, I have had a few custom-made products. Getting an item tailored means the item designed is fitted to your uniqueness. Growing up, I heard from my father that no one could do what you do like you do. My father was always encouraging my individuality and the importance of being true to myself. We are all unique. Saul of Tarsus once stated, "we are God's masterpiece," meaning we are His work of art. As humans, we are unlike mass production. We are custom made and our unique design is for His purpose.

Don Clifton once wrote a book about what's right with people. A 40-year study about human strengths yielded a language of 34 common talent themes. A book entitled Discover Your CliftonStrengths, or mostly known as StrengthsFinder, helps you discover your top talents or strengths. In my study of his work, I have learned that our top 5 talents, regardless of order, are 1 in 278,000. Our top 5 talents in the same order are 1 in 33.39 million, and our top 10 talents in the same order are 1 in 447 trillion. There are over 7.4 billion people globally, and there is a 1 in 447 trillion chance we are the same. Custom-made! We will dive more into Strengths later in the book, but what I wanted to convey is like a snowflake, you are unique. To echo the words of King David, "fearfully and wonderfully made," we are. Yet, comparing yourself to others can lead to feelings of inferiority. It is often subtle and may arise when we minimize ourselves and lift others on a pedestal.

## Feelings of inferiority

Feelings of inferiority can repeatedly manifest in our lives and affect our relationships, performance, and self-perception. It is when we keep comparing ourselves with others and always end up selling ourselves short. We tend to major in the minor flaws and minor in the major strengths. This outlook leads to emotions of hopelessness, anger, resentment, anxiety, and a host of other feelings. Here are a few tips to overcome feelings of inferiority:

- **Stop Wanting To Be Like Others.** Many times our feelings of inferiority are rooted in the desire to be someone else. These feelings make you want to be someone you are not. Others can be guides; others may have characteristics we may adopt, but ultimately be true to yourself.

- **Stop Worrying About What Others Think.** We sometimes find problems with ourselves based on if others see us as good enough. This is stinky thinking and not healthy at all. Only your opinion of yourself truly matters.

- **Positive Self-Talk.** For many years, I have said one who listens to self is foolish; one who talks to self is wise, which may seem counterintuitive, but the truth is, "self" will tell you many things, but you have to remind yourself who you are and whose you are. Locate the negative thoughts and replace them with positive, self-affirming communication. Consider making a list of five to ten things you love about yourself and hang it where you can see it daily. You will be amazed at the increased self-worth and overall confidence.

Being your true self is very empowering and relaxing. Overcome your need to be like others or impress others. No matter what you do, some people will be impressed, and others won't. Why worry about it? You're a wonderful person. Allow yourself to be that person every day. Remember, God has made you unique. Therefore, like David wrote, "I praise you, for I am fearfully and wonderfully made. Wonderful are your works;"

## Here's an action item:

In your journal, write down what makes you unique.

Also, make a list of five to ten things you love about yourself.

## Personal Affirmation

I am fearfully and wonderfully made. I am full of complexities, and I love who I am becoming. I will not compare myself to others but will compare myself to me. I will review the list of things that I love about myself and make it a point to recite them daily. I am empowered. I am free from seeking other's approval and trying to impress them. Today, I celebrate my uniqueness.

# 6

# Friends, How Many Of Us Have Them?

I never imagined that a 20 plus year friendship could begin in a bathroom. But it did. Although pretty close friends for many years, it was freshmen year in the bathroom at the University of Texas that our friendship took a profound and severe turn. A series of life decisions led Keven, Ray, and I onto the bathroom floor, making a pact with spoken and unspoken words. It was out of our vulnerability that a deep friendship was launched. In her book Dare To Lead, Brene Brown defines vulnerability as the *emotion we experience during uncertainty, risk, and emotional exposure.* Uncertain about what tomorrow would bring, it was out of that moment we dared to always be there for each other. Years have gone by, and many life events later, we are still best friends. It is not that we talk daily, but these are men I will gladly die for, and whenever we connect, I/we are emotionally exposed. Although I have added other people into my circle, these men remain close! We found in each other a kindred spirit.

I think by now in our lives, we are aware of the different types of friends: social media, associate, classmate, close and inner circles. However, I wonder if we are mindful of the importance of a tribe of people that aids in you becoming the best version of yourself.

Surround yourself with a tribe that requires more of you than you are willing to give. Think about it; some of your most influential teachers, coaches, etc., are those who wanted more of you than you were initially willing to give. In doing so, they were able to pull greatness out of you. I have made some incredible friendships; I would even venture into saying that my tribes are all unique and push me considerably. Whether it's Da Crew, The Pack, or other tribes, I am grateful for the much-needed push to become better. As we continue to discuss friendships, it is also important to expose a few myths about friendships.

## Myth #1 You never disagree

Quite the contrary, real friendships are those you continue to show up for even when you can't control the outcome. There have been countless times in my deep friendships we have disagreed. That is what makes our friendship so unique; it builds character. Friendships don't mean you agree with everything said or done; it just means you'll do life together despite those minor disagreements.

## Myth #2 You have to be in constant communication

On the DiSC personality profile, I would be considered a super extrovert. Even in StrengthsFinder, my number one strength is Winning Others Over and Connectedness. I love people and love to socialize. However, one of the myths about friends is that you have to communicate every day continually. Now there may be seasons when this happens organically, but it is not always the case.

This doesn't mean never reach out to your friends or wait around for them to contact you as they need you. It is the freedom to be you, freedom to pour into self and fill your tank up so that when you are connected with and to others, you have something of value to give them as well.

## Myth #3 Friendships Are Forever

I am not much of a gardener, but those who are often say they love the dirt between their nails and oneness with Earth. Although not much of a gardener, I do see many life lessons from the ground. One life lesson reminds us of friendships. There are times in life when a plant has outgrown its pot and needs a new surrounding. Like a plant not meant to live in its environment forever, all friendships are not meant to last forever.

Andy Stanley once wrote, "the great thing about having friends who share your season of life is that you have so much in common." However, there comes a season when there is no common ground, and in fact, remaining in the pot will stifle the growth.

There have been friends in my life that are no longer considered a friend or someone in my inner circle, but it doesn't mean we become unfriendly.

## Myth #4 Broken Friendships Can't Be Mended

As we have already learned, no friendship is free from conflict. However, what do you do when conflict has pushed you away? First, you decide is it wise to maintain the friendship? Mending or reconciliation is always right. Even if you choose that the friendship has run its course, you should always seek to mend broken relationships. However, just because you clear the air doesn't mean you have to "do life with them."

## Myth #5 All Friends Support

There are times in our lives when we launch new endeavors and the people we want to show up for us the most are not present. It's possible that your friends may be supporting you in unique ways. Maybe it's through prayer, referrals, or listening ears. However, don't always think the lack of presence equals the lack of support. However, when lack of support is evident, you can be bitter or better; your choice. The lack of love, support, or care in an area hurts, but it should increase your grind and the seeds of support you sow.

# How to Keep Good Friendships?

### 1. Accept your friends for who they are

Acceptance is the capacity to recognize that others have a right to be their unique selves. That means having a right to feel and think the way they are wired. When you accept people for who they are, you take them as they are and let go of your desire to change them.

### 2. Treat friends the way you want to be treated

Known as the golden rule, "treat others how you want to be treated" is also a lesson in sowing and reaping. Whatever you sow is what you will reap, and if you treat people a certain way, it will come back to you. One thing about sowing and reaping to note: Whatever you sow, you reap more. When you plant a seed, it has the potential of becoming an orchard. Therefore, we should be mindful of how we treat others and how we speak about, think about, and feel about them.

### 3. Remember to say thank you

There is not only a personal benefit to saying thank you, but it also makes others feel appreciated. It is the simplest way to say "you are appreciated" and provide inner happiness and motivation. It indicates that you recognize their effort and may even encourage them to go the extra mile.

### 4. Remain faithful and trustworthy

I think loyalty is perhaps the most prized characteristic in any relationship. A loyal friend is someone who makes the relationship they have with you their priority! To prioritize friendships means knowing when to go to your friend, even when they haven't asked you to. It's having the ability to receive confidential information and allowing it to go into a vault.

**5. Don't keep records of wrongs**

Agape love is selfless, sacrificial, unconditional love. It is the highest form of love, and one of the most quoted passages in the Bible about love is found in 1 Corinthians 13. One critical statement about love is "love keeps no record of wrong." True friendship is a friendship based on love; this doesn't keep a record of wrongdoing, even though imperfect people make plenty of mistakes.

**6. Do not smother your friend**

Along the lines of loyalty, you don't have to talk to them every day knowing they have others friends. Be glad they have others friends besides you. You know you have a loyal friend if you don't have to talk to them every day, but rather when you spend time apart and when you finally meet, you feel a sense of belonging as if you never missed a beat.

## Here's an action item:

Who is in your inner circle? Consider writing a thank you letter of appreciation for their friendship.

### Personal Affirmation

Today, I choose valuable relationships. I will be cautious of those I add to my inner circle. I seek to be a courageous friend and will not shy from being vulnerable. I will keep no record of wrongdoings and will mend relationships that I cherish deeply.

Today, I choose to remain a faithful and loyal friend and accept my friends for who they are as I desire the same.

# 7

## Forgiving Yourself

I once heard the story of how hunters place a banana into a tree trunk with an opening the size of a monkey's open hand. Once the monkey sees the banana, he puts his hand into the tree and grabs the banana, and as he pulls it out, his clenched fist is too big to be pulled out. So enamored by the banana, the monkey will not let go, and thus the capturers come and take the monkey captive. I believe there are life lessons in this story and one crucial word: attachment.

Often, when someone has wronged us, we are faced with a choice to forgive or hold on. When we choose not to let go, we are attaching ourselves to that thing, targeted at ourselves or others. Let's take a look as to why it is essential to forgive yourself.

## The 3 Most Important Steps to Forgiving Yourself

Many times we are good with forgiving others but have a difficult time forgiving our missteps. Often the thought of letting yourself or others down makes you feel rotten. But it would help if you allowed the sun to shine again. Has it been challenging to do that?

Here is a 3-step process that can help you forgive yourself and move on with your life.

First of all, you must come face to face with your mistake. Confront it! In all circumstances, take responsibility for your error. Come face to face with it and acknowledge where you stumbled. As painful as it might be, this is the first step to forgiving yourself: no blame game, no passing the buck. Own your mistake. Quite honestly, it may prove beneficial to look into a mirror and say aloud what you did. By doing so, it helps you to realize making mistakes is okay. It may also prove prudent to speak with a therapist who can assist with releasing feelings that may be tied down inside. Secondly, it is crucial to accept your imperfections.

Therefore, be kind to yourself and remind yourself, "I am human." Life is about progression, not perfection, so be kind to yourself. Now, this is not a license to bask in those imperfections but rather an opportunity to continue working on yourself by strengthening your character. Lastly, stop the attachment and challenge yourself to be and do better. After accepting and analyzing your missteps, it's time to work on them. Ask your supportive friends and family to help you on your journey. Remember that no man is an island, and making things right might not happen overnight. What's important is that you forgive yourself and commit to turning things around.

I recall making a mistake once as a leader. Something that was asked by other leaders, and I failed to get accomplished. I owned it, resolved it, and then asked myself what I can do to ensure this doesn't happen again. So I created a weekly tracker. Several sections on this tracker included a checklist of the crucial things needed to get accomplished daily/weekly, significant appointments, and any additions as directed by senior leadership. In asking myself what went wrong and making the necessary adjustments, I was able to rectify the issue and increase my productivity by implementing a fail-safe.

In conclusion we all make mistakes, but learning and growing, as a result, is vital to our overall success. Be sure to extend forgiveness to yourself in the process. Remember the words of Roy Williams, "A smart man makes a mistake, learns from it, and never makes that mistake again. But a wise man finds a smart man and learns from him how to avoid the mistake altogether."

Today I encourage you to be wise, and if you haven't reached that level yet, at least be smart.

## Here's an action item:

In your journal answer this:

1) What are 3 things for which I should forgive myself?
2) How would my life change if I were better at forgiving myself?
3) Who else should I forgive?

### Personal Affirmation

Everyone deserves forgiveness, so I find it easy not only to forgive others but myself. I embrace my errors and strive to grow from them. I have the power to release myself from past mistakes. Today, I am free of guilt, embarrassment and full of self-love. I am becoming the best version of myself, and I cannot cling to the past, so I let go. I am free of doubt.

# 8

# Creating Clarity: Life Mapping

This chapter repurposed and modified for this book, initially published in Conversations: Developing An Intimate Dialogue With God (Westbow Press, 2014)

*"Take A Risk. Take A Chance. Make A Change. And Breakaway"* – Kelly Clarkson

People will often find themselves rushing into their 30s, 40s, and sometimes into their 50s before they begin to gain a sense of purpose. I am convinced that the older one gets, the more the question of "why I exist" becomes more important to answer. Many people find themselves working and chasing the "American dream" or "chasing the jones" family (whoever they are) and never taking into consideration the reason they are on this planet. What is the wealthiest place on Earth? Quite possibly the most affluent place on the Earth is in the graveyards, whereby you will find countless people who did not accomplish or reach their full potential.

Potential is untapped power…it is things you have yet to do….it is all that you have not yet become….Myles Munroe once said, "potential is the sum of who you are that you have yet to reveal." I have known what I wanted to do in life for a long time, but as I got older, I became more fine-tuned. When I turned 25, I understood the value of creating a map for my life. This map would assist me in determining what I should engage in or not. My life map enables me to "take a risk, take a chance, make a change, and breakaway" from some things.

Even when you have to do specific jobs to get by, for now, make sure you never lose sight of why you are here and how you are to fulfill that duty. Or maybe you should "take a risk, take a chance, make a change, and breakaway." Having a life map also helps you identify people who should be in your life (i.e., relationships, friends, etc.). Thus, you may have people you need to break away from because they possibly hinder you in pursuing your progression.

A life map consists of three main components: Purpose, Vision, and Mission statements.

## Here is my life map....

Vision (what I envision?) Since a little kid, I have always envisioned bringing life to dead places. A guiding principle for me found in Isaiah 35:1, which says, "the desert and the parched land will be glad, the wilderness will rejoice and blossom..." My mother and father named me Robert, which means shining with fame, or bright. Even as a child, I brought light to dark places. I am light, and wherever I go, light shows up.

Mission (What I am to accomplish?) To fulfill my purpose by evangelizing, edifying (building up), encouraging, and equipping others to affect change in their world. If I can evangelize to the lost, build up those weak, encourage people in their walk, and prepare all to accomplish their purpose, I, in essence, achieve my goal.

Purpose (why I exist?) I live to bring God glory (make Him famous) and affect change in my world: 1) as a pattern of the glorious truth (1 Tim 1:16; 1 Tim 4:12); and 2) as a witness (2 Tim. 1:8) I knew from an early age that I was created for more than what my surrounding dictated. I have known God would put me before people great and small.

## What about you?

Have you thought about your life map? If not, here are three questions to help lead you. What guides you (values, morals, etc.)? What is your passion (heartbeat, desires, etc.)? Why do you believe you exist? What unique gifting or talents do you possess? Will you maximize your potential? I implore you not to rob our generation of the wealth and resource God has placed within you! Remember, sometimes you have to "take a risk, take a chance, make a change, and breakaway" to navigate your way through your life. Taking the time to discover your life map will give direction to life, help release your potential and ultimately help filter decisions.

## Here's an action item:

In your journal work through these questions:
What guides you? What is your passion? Why do you believe you exist? What unique gifts/talents fo you possess?

## Personal Affirmation

Today I realize the difference between dreams and reality is my action. I will allow my life map to help direct me. My purpose speaks to why I exist, and I filter all activities through this. I will release my potential daily and maximize each moment afforded to me. I will not drift, but strive for greatness, because my life map directs me.

# 9

## Set On Fire

Some people would argue that the driving force behind all things is passion. Although things can be created without passion, it isn't easy to sustain life without it. Passion gives many people the excitement to wake up in the morning and take on the world. I once heard that without passion, life becomes boring, relationships are mundane, and you don't blaze new trails. Without passion, life lacks direction, force, intensity, and acuteness. However, with passion, a young lad name Demond Lee would be spent dreaming of flying airplanes and, when he grew to maturity, accomplish his dream. With passion, a young girl named Jessica

Richardson will dream of dancing and grow up moving through a set series of movements with or without music. Passion is a deep-seated God-given emotion ready to be directed in a specific area. Remember John Wesley once said, "when you set yourself on fire, people love to come and see you burn."

Have you lost your passion? Are you searching for ways to rekindle the flame that was once lit in your life? Here are a few practical ways to restore your passion:

## Make sure you have a fireplace

One of the hardest things for one log to do is to sustain. When I am on the grill BarBecueing, one of the first things I do is make sure all of my charcoals are in a close pile together. It is not until after they have fully lit do I spread them out. I believe there is a lesson in this for us; we should gather together with other passionate people to rekindle our fire and have a safe place for us to ignite. Passion needs to be fed to keep blazing, and the power of passionate people will affect our flames.

## Your Fire Needs To Be Stoked

An older man, Paul, writes to his protege Timothy and tells him that he needed to stoke his fire. Paul didn't doubt that fire was blazing on the inside but reminded him that he needed to keep the fire alive. Fan into the flame is for you to "fan the embers into flame and not let them die out." Whatever gift God has given you to exercise, keep kindling that fire afresh and watch "people come and see you burn." Stoke your flame by allowing the wind of the Holy Spirit to breathe on you.

## Focus Your Fire

Have you ever seen a person passionate without direction? They are burning up everything. The devastation caused by unbridled passion is evident in the examples of wildfires that sweep across plains. In World of Warcraft, a fire that is focused increases your damage and the critical strike of your unique abilities. Paul writes to the Romans and expounds on how many of his brethren had zeal (passion) but lacked knowledge. They, in essence, were all over the place, thus in their passion, they lacked spiritual wisdom and enlightenment even to the point of persecuting and murdering our Savior. Focus your fire by seeking the time with your firestarter for understanding, refinement, and direction.

## Take Time To Rest

We will discuss rest more in a later chapter, however,

remember that tending to fires and burning for a cause can lead to burnout. We must take time amid our fireworks to rest awhile and rejuvenate so that the firestarter can revive us for continual service. Be sure to pull away from the crowds for a time of one-on-one with the fire starter.

## Here's an action item:

Take some time to discover if you have lost your flame, and what would it look like to blaze again?

### Personal Affirmation

Today, I live on fire. My passions will help guide me. Living on fire allows me to live authentically. I realize that when I am on fire, others will not only come and watch me burn but will join me living authentically.

# 10

# Healthier Life Journey

Reaching your full potential is dependent on the creation and maintenance of a healthy self-image and lifestyle. It is virtually impossible to be successful in life if you don't have a healthy self-image. It is also hard to accomplish the things you want to in life without a healthy journey. The way you view yourself is either uplifting or a hindrance. Despite childhood experiences, past failings, or current level of self-esteem, you can possess a healthy self-image.

It is vital to avoid underestimating the impact of your self-image on other areas of your life. To reach your full potential, you must respect yourself and believe you can do great things. You must value yourself and watch your self-image flourish. Here are a few practical steps:

1. **Subdue** any limiting beliefs. We enjoy things in life, but due to limiting beliefs, we give up too soon. What are they? We all have that negative voice telling us what we cannot do. Make a list of how that belief is negatively impacting your life. Now, focus on how removing this belief will improve your life.

2. **See** the small victories. We often celebrate the climb to the mountaintop; however, it's accumulating small incremental steps that make the end possible. How do you climb Mt. Everest? By taking one step at a time. Any progress is worthy of recognition. Significant successes are the culmination of many more minor successes.

3. **Strive** daily toward your ideal self. We all have a vision of the person we'd like to be. That ideal version of ourselves might seem too far away even to consider, but take a small step each day. Each slight improvement will raise your self-image. Start today by listing all the qualities you'd like to have.

4. **Supplant** self-talk. I used to say a lot, "he who listens to himself is foolish, but he who talks to himself is wise." The reality is that we all talk to ourselves. You're not the only one! The greatest thing about this is that we can control what we say to ourselves. Is your self-

talk positive or negative? Negative self-talk chips away at your feelings of self-worth. Be kind to yourself. Be promising, positive, and patient.

5. **Start** eating better. Healthy behaviors are essential in all facets of our lives. When developing healthy eating behaviors, you are planning and preparing well. As another person once said, "those who fail to plan, plan to fail," so plan well. Planning well includes:

-Setting goals.

– Creating a meal plan.

– Writing a shopping list.

– Cooking in bulk or cooking the night before.

6. **Strengthen** your body. I wrote an entire book about the benefits of working out, it's called Wake Pray Train (a must read) and I would encourage you to pick that book up. It is a interactive faith and fitness guide with workouts, meal plans, and more. However, for the purpose of this book, it's highly important to not only focus on emotional, spiritual, and nutritional health but also physical fitness. Being physically fit helps with mental clarity, daily energy, focus, and longevity of life.

Ultimately you have to change your attitude towards food and your goals, maintain a positive focus, and have realistic expectations if you will be successful in eating more healthy.

Begin to build a healthy self-image today. Regardless of your past or current impressions of yourself, you can learn to view yourself in a more positive light. A healthy self-image is a springboard to happiness and success. Focus on the small victories in your life and be proud of your progress. You deserve to be successful and happy. I have uploaded on my website a highly effective daily productivity guide I have used for over 5 years now. It helps me remain focused and productive. Remember that small and steady builds momentum, make your healthy a nonnegotiable thing.

## Here's an action item:

Grab my book Wake Pray Train as a valuable resource.

### Personal Affirmation

My healthy self-image is a springboard to happiness and success, thus, I will be mindful of healthier choices. Today I focus on the small victories that lead to the monumental ones. I deserve to be happy and it starts with my decision to choose me. I choose longevity of life. I choose healthy friendships. I choose to remain focus on my goals.

# 11

## Serve Others

In our quest to become our most authentic selves, another valuable characteristic is serving others. As it relates to serving or helping others, I once read an old Chinese Proverb that says, "If you want happiness for an hour, take a nap. If you want happiness for a day, go fishing. If you want happiness for a year, inherit a fortune. If you want happiness for a lifetime, help somebody."

When we serve others, there are many benefits, including making your heart feel good. However, serving doesn't just make your heart feel good; research has shown that physiological and psychological factors like extending our lives, reducing depression, and even lowering blood pressure. When we put others' needs before our own, we are sowing seeds of happiness, and therefore, we reap. This harvest is evident in our relationships as we strengthen our bonds and enrich the lives of others.

I implemented a monthly giveback Sunday at a church I served for several years. It was a day we would call Mission Sunday. Mission Sunday was a day we wouldn't have an actual church service but go out and be the church to our community. We adequately dubbed it: Displaying A.R.K, which means Acts of Redeemed Kindness, a play on the name of the church Ark Bible Fellowship. We did everything from washing cars, paid for groceries, cleaned parks, and more. This monthly event was one of the highlights of our service. I often would say that if you need joy, plant joy in others' lives and watch how joy is reaped in yours. If you need finances, sow finances, and if you need love, plant it. This is what serving is all about; it is sowing seeds into the lives of others. It's how we become the best versions of ourselves.

## So how do we start...

First, realize that you were given what you have, not

for just yourself but for others. I believe our talents, abilities, and gifts were given not only for us but also for others' enrichment. I say often that the world's wealthiest place was the cemetery because it was the place many died without reaching their full potential. I have this phrase I often say, "don't rob your generation of the wealth within you." Serve others!

Secondly, you have to make helping others a priority. Have you ever thought, "I don't have enough time to volunteer or serve," but when you did, you were so glad you did? Indeed, we are all busy with life. But how often have you said this but spent countless hours watching the same reruns or highlights on ESPN? We have to prioritize the things that we value.

Lastly, you need to exhibit love. My father used to say, "that you can give without loving, but you cannot love without giving." Think about it; one of the most famous verses is John 3:16, which says, "for God so loved the world that He gave..." Serving others is proof that we love. Gestures as simple as a compliment, running an errand, paying for dinner may mean more to people than you may ever know. And perhaps the best benefit of service is the chance of that person paying it forward.

## Here's an action item:

How can you pay it forward? Think of ways to serve others and act today!

### Personal Affirmation

I have been created for more than myself. I choose to give myself to others. My gifts will be shared with others and I will prioritize others. I will love through giving and spark a culture of service.

# 12

# Refueling (Rest)

Each day we use something important. For many of us, it is a lifeline! Studies have shown that about 65% of men/women combined have a fear. It is the fear of losing or being without their cell phone, also known as nomophobia. You know that feeling when you reach into your pocket and go into immediate panic mode, checking everywhere trying to locate it. Your heart races, your stomach turns, and your brain kicks into overdrive, trying to remember where you last laid it. It is because we use these small devices for everything. We walk around all day texting, talking, and tracking things. However, by the end of the day, we have dwindled the battery. It needs new power. What do you do? You connect it to power and charge it. Many of us understand the absolute importance of connecting the phone to the correct plug and laying them down to rest because it will not work if we don't. However, many of us don't understand the importance of proper rest for ourselves.

Daily I lead teams of exciting professionals, and one of the main things I try to preach is self-care. I emphasize that taking good care of yourself is one of the best things we can do for ourselves, our families, jobs, etc. It is far from being selfish; it's a sacrifice that benefits everyone around. The greatest man to ever walk this Earth, namely Jesus, took time often to pull away from the crowd and rest.

For this book, I want to focus on two significant ways to refuel: Self and Spiritual.

## Self- Care Tips

Well-balanced rest is a sign of effective stewardship. It realizes you have been giving only one body, one mind, one heart, one life to live, and without adequately managing rest, you will mismanage those things and end your life abruptly. When our lives end abruptly, it reduces the impact that we have on this Earth, and thus we are not becoming the best version of ourselves possible. Our goal should be to get replenished so that we can pour ourselves again and again. Wells are exciting. As water flows out, new and freshwater come in, thus keeping the water healthy. Good self-care means that you must learn to attend to your own needs. Sleep is one of the best ways to do so. When we get proper sleep, our lives get a daily reset to take on tomorrow's challenges. It can also be prudent to set the alarm reminding you to take regular breaks, even if it is just a walk around the block or an uninterrupted snack. Often, stepping away will energize you to work more efficiently when you return. I would also suggest things like meditation, breathing, guided imagery, and massages to aid in replenishing yourself.

## Spiritual Tank

Up until this point, I haven't spoken much about your spirituality. This may be a section you love or hard to wrestle with. However, without a spiritual awakening, your quest for a life fully authentic may come up a little short. We are trichotomous beings, meaning we are Spirit, soul, and body. Without fueling the spiritual tank, you will be consistently missing the mark. The Bible makes it clear that those who have placed faith in Jesus for salvation are in the process of becoming more conformed to the image of Jesus (Sanctification). Jesus is the perfect man and the prime example of one who lived the best version of himself. We should strive to be like Him daily. However, the process of becoming more like Him (sanctification) doesn't happen by accident; instead, we are to make ourselves available to the perfecting work of the Holy Spirit. Spiritual disciplines are exercises or activities that one engages in habitually to bring them closer to God, refuel their spiritual tanks, and becoming more like Jesus in character and conduct.

Dallas Willard categorizes these as Disciplines of Abstinence (1 Pet 2:11) and Disciplines of Engagement (Mark 2:11). For a detailed look at this, grab a copy of his book *The Spirit of the Disciplines*. Here is a quick look at 10 of them:

1) Prayer – in which one spends time talking to God (Dan. 6:10; Col. 4:2)

2) Meditation – in which one contemplates God's word, or other things worthy of such attention (Ps. 1:1-2; Ph. 4:8).

3) Fasting – usually accompanied with prayer, in which one abstains from food (Neh. 1:4; Acts. 13:2-3; 14:23)

4) Singing – through which one can praise God and be edified (Ps. 71:23; Acts 16:25)

5) Giving – by which we can please God and be blessed (Heb 13:16; Acts 20:35)

6) Assembling – where we can encourage one another Ps. 122:1; Heb 10:24-25)

7) Hospitality – showing kindness to strangers, which often results in a blessing (Heb 13:2)

8) Teaching – which usually benefits the teacher more than the student (Heb. 5:12-14)

9) Service – where we see God's compassion and love are flowing through us to those in need. (Col. 3:22-24; Matt. 20:25-28)

10) Bible Reading – allowing the words of God to strengthen and encourage our faith (2 Tim. 3:16-17)

## Monitor Your Fuel

The technology for cell phones has increased over the years. The capacity to do more is present, but the cell's dilemma is doing too much at once and causing the battery to decrease quickly. When this happens, we clear apps running in the background, reduce the number of notifications, or give the phone break it needs. This is true of our lives as well. First of all, lower your expectations of others by starting your day off, bringing your expectations closer to zero. Secondly, receive everything that happens to you as filtered through the fingertips of God's love toward you. This means that nothing happens that God is unaware of, and though all things that happen to us are not good, they all work together for our good. However, only valid for those who love God and are called according to His purpose (Romans 8:28). Third, when we are upset by things that happen, we take the opportunity to engage in spiritual disciplines of prayer, worship, and bible reading. For spiritual disciplines gives us the needed spiritual refueling to undergo any day. Lastly, rest in God daily while listening attentively as to what He is telling you.

## Here's an action item:

Adopt a discipline each day for a week. Journal what you did, how you felt and any reflections.

### Personal Affirmation

Today, I take ownership of my self care. My self-care benefits everyone around me and affects positive change. I flow from a full spiritual tank, because I choose to rest in God. I am refreshed, I am refueled, I am revived.

Rise Slay Eat • 69

# 13

# Center S.T.A.G.E.

During my high school years, I loved Drama. I remember during one recital, I performed the Shakespeare monologue All The World's A Stage. Although this monologue appears to be about the theater, in essence, he sees life as a drama acted out on a stage and outlined the journey of a man from birth to the grave. If the world's a stage and all humans players, how are you taking center stage in your life?

As this book concludes, the goal was to learn practical ways to become the best version of yourself and progress towards taking Center S.T.A.G.E. in your life.

When I speak about S.T.A.G.E., I am explicitly talking about how your Strengths, Temperaments, Abilities, Gifts, and Experiences can propel you to not just be on the stage of life, but in fact, become the leading player. In my coaching, I take people on a deeper dive into their S.T.A.G.E. but let's whet your appetite here.

## S.T.A.G.E.: Strengths

Many people in life operate from a place of weakness. A great deal of our time in life we spend on how we can make our weaknesses stronger. Although there is value in improving our areas of opportunity, the real value is living from a place of strength. When you focus on your strengths or do what you do best, you will significantly impact the quality of life and career success. People who operate from a place of strength are those who grow more quickly than trying to focus on weaknesses.

Have you ever noticed there are things you enjoyed doing and other things you do not? We all have things we do more naturally, and then some things are more natural for others. Don Clifton, the mastermind behind StrengthsFinder, identified 34 different themes that describe most people's styles. In his conclusions, building upon these themes are the keys to being happy and prosperous. Four main domains house each theme: strategic thinking, relationship building, influencing, and executing; each theme also comprises of roughly eight strengths. Once you know your themes or strengths, it becomes easier to adapt (i.e., life, career, relationships) to align with the things you are strong at doing. I remember having a conversation with a coworker once about my ability to be organized; although I was pretty skilled, it took an extreme amount of effort to do so. In my younger years, my father would say something like, "focus on your strengths and staff your weaknesses." We don't always afford that luxury, but our lives are better for it and those around us when we operate from a place of strength. I would encourage you to look at his book StrengthsFinder and many online resources to help identify your strengths.

Strengths I believe I have from assessments:

| 1. | 2. | 3. | 4. | 5. |
|---|---|---|---|---|

## S.T.A.G.E.: Temperaments

What is temperament? Temperament is a combination of genetic traits that subconsciously affect our human behavior. It is the source of what makes people extrovert, introvert, task-oriented, or people-oriented. There are many assessments and profiles to determine your inherent characteristics from Meyers Brigg, Personality Plus, and DiSC. Over the years, I have learned more about the DiSC profile philosophy, and without going too in-depth, I want to share a few basics about temperaments.

## What is DiSC?

The DiSC is a highly acclaimed personal assessment tool used by many people to boost teamwork, collaboration, and productivity in the workplace. It is also vital in knowing about yourself. DiSC stands for Dominance, Influence, Steadfastness, and Conscientiousness, but I use Director (D), Influencer (i), Sister Hen (S), and Mr. Calculator (C) for quickly remembering. Those with D style, or directors, tend to be fast-paced and outspoken individuals. They exude a lot of self-confidence, directness, and forcefulness. When being self-aware, they should consider they tend to be seen as having a lack of concern for others and impatient individuals. The Influences are also fast-paced individuals who are more people-focused, unlike the more task-oriented directors. Influencers are motivated by recognition and tend to fear rejection. Mr. Calculator is more methodical and logic-focused. This individual is precise, analytical, and very reserved, yet often overly critical. Lastly, Sister Hen is a patient, caring, and calm listener. Although she can be highly accommodating and indecisive, this personality is great at empathizing. There are many places online to explore more and fine-tune your character, so I would recommend you do so. However, for this book, I wanted to give a brief overview.

My DiSC personality profile is:

## S.T.A.G.E.: Abilities & Gifts

Although I haven't mentioned spirituality much to this point, I am a firm believer that as we become the best version of ourselves, we awaken spiritually as well. Gifts, by the very mention of the term, are something we receive unearned. I believe that at birth, you were given things that are unique to you. I think that everyone has been given natural talents or abilities to use for the glory of God. No matter where you are located as you read this, you are incredibly talented and gifted. Now talent is something you were born with – like a musical ability to play an instrument. However, only those who are awakened spiritually are given spiritual gifts to expand God's Kingdom. Now there are natural gifts and spiritual ones. Although we are not gifted the same, we are all gifted in some way or another and extremely valuable to God and the world.

My Current Vocation is:
Other Jobs/skills I have experience in:

I feel my most valuable asset is:
My Spiritual Gifts are:

## S.T.A.G.E.: Experiences

We have all heard it said that "experience is the best teacher," why we all realize that our experiences shape us, we are shaped by every experience one way or another. Every experience! Even an experience that is not monumental will change us. One of the most overlooked factors in discovering self is how past experiences, particularly our hurts, pains, and disappointments, mold us into who we are. As you begin to look at your experiences, please ask these questions.

**Spiritual** *Experiences*: What are the meaningful decisions or times I have had with God? What did I learn?

_____

**Painful** *Experiences*: What have I learned from my pain?

_____

**Education** *Experiences*: What did I learn during school? What were my favorite subjects?

This book has been a journey towards taking steps to become the best version of yourself. In doing so, you will begin to take Center S.T.A.G.E. of your story and live/leave a legacy for the world to enjoy. Suppose you are interested in digging deeper into S.T.A.G.E. discovery. In that case, I invite you to join me at SE7EN University, which is an interactive online training program that leads people to self-mastery.

Whether you need help in personal, leadership, or spiritual development, SE7EN University will challenge you to grow and become the best version of yourself possible. I invite you to join others with our on-demand audio, email, and video teachings leading people to self-mastery.

I want to end this book differently. Usually, I would conclude, but I want to end this book as an affirmation. To allow these practical tips to take root, I pray this book and final affirmation found in the next chapter will strengthen your journey.

# 14

## Be Adventurous: Life Is Good

### Final Affirmation

Today, I Rise, Slay and Eat. I become the best version of myself and take Center S.T.A.G.E. These principles will strengthen me daily.

I am filled with a spirit of adventure. This year I summon up my courage to pursue the things I want. I will take sensible risks. I will evaluate the consequences of my actions and learn from those experiences.

I will show my enthusiasm *and greet each day with a smile.*

I will take advantage of each opportunity available to me and even create my own. I will grow wiser and stronger as a result of it.

Today, I let go of the past. My future is determined by the choices that I make today. I forgive myself and others for past disappointments. *I am eager to make a fresh start.*

I stand up to challenges and obstacles. I focus on what I have to gain. I remind myself of the rewards in store for me when I work hard and think strategically. I will be a better friend and surround myself with people who add to my life and not takeaway. Positive role models will be sought out. I rely on their guidance and encouragement as I dare to break out of my comfort zone.

I will reach my final destination and take Center S.T.A.G.E. of my life. My gifts will make room for me, and my experiences teach me well. The world is my stage, and I shine brightly. I refuse to shrink back, but will shine brightly in every area.

*I move ahead with confidence, and sometimes I move in silence.* I will enjoy the journey this year as I strive towards fulfilling my goals, passion, and purpose.

Author, Speaker, and Transformation Specialist. Robert wrote his first book entitled Conversations: Developing An Intimate Dialogue With God in 2014. Robert has an extreme passion to see people grow spiritually, naturally and physically as seen by his 20+ years of experience as a 'trainer. One of his generation's most creative bible expositors delivering high energy, creativity and in-depth instruction to each presentation. He is a graduate of University of North Texas and received a Masters in Christian Education from Dallas Theological Seminary. He is motivated and inspired to help people become the best version of themselves.

www.ingramcontent.com/pod-product-compliance
Lightning Source LLC
Chambersburg PA
CBHW071411290426
44108CB00014B/1772